Roman Dirge's

LENORE

COOTIES

Written and illustrated by
Roman Dirge

TITAN BOOKS

LENORE: COOTIES
ISBN 1 84576 169 3
ISBN-13 978184576169 1

Published by Titan Books
A division of
Titan Publishing Group Ltd
144 Southwark Street
London SE1 OUP

Book designed by Mark Cox

This edition first published: July 2006
1 3 5 7 9 10 8 6 4 2

Visit Roman Dirge at www.spookyland.com
www.titanbooks.com

Other books by
Roman Dirge

LENORE: NOOGIES
LENORE: WEDGIES

What did you think of this book?
We love to hear from our readers.
Please email us at:
readerfeedback@titanemail.com,
or write to us at the
above address.

CONTENTS

by Roman Dirge

Hello there…

Ah,
what a loooong gooey road this whole journey has been. When I published my first *Lenore* comic in 1992, there was no such entity-thing as "goth comics". No special section for my work to be exiled to in comic book stores. It was and still is just doing what I've always done and loved, penning the continuing adventures of a cute little dead girl who has the brain capacity about that of an old retarded squirrel. It's strange. Lenore has evolved into an almost real being to me. When I sit down to write each issue, it really writes itself. I can hear her voice in my head telling me what she'd say in every situation. Apart from the obvious indications that I may have some sort of mental disorder, what with voices in my head, this otherwise bodes well for me. It's like I can just sit back, drink beer, quest with my level 60 Warlock, and Lenore writes her own books. If she'd just learn to draw herself now, I'd be home free. I could retire and return to the exciting world of close up magic, whereas I'd once again be able to utter such phrases, to people trying to eat, as,

"Behold, the coin was in this hand but now it is gone… And is in this OTHER hand now!" and then they'd go, "Yeah, that's… that's great. Can you tell our waiter we need more napkins?" And then I'd look at them, a magical gleam in my eye, and I'd say, "Yeah, ok."

What's my point in all this? I have no idea. All I know is that whatever else I do with my life, I will forever be remembered for birthing a stinky little zombie child with worms and I'm totally ok with that, especially since my chances of becoming an underwear model seem to be becoming more and more slim.

This compilation of the last four issues is special to me. *Noogies*, the first trade paperback, has a special place in my dark heart because it was the beginning of the adventure. Most of the tales within were reprints of the original *Lenore* comics from 1992. They're funny and short, BUT I really couldn't draw that well back then and I also didn't have any direction as to where it was all headed. I was all pimples and just out of high school. It's an odd feeling to have your old work being reprinted over and over and people will see it for the first time now and that is their original impression of you. I guess what I'm saying is that I'm a little embarrassed of the crappy art from back then but I stand by "the funny" of it. *Wedgies*, the second compilation book, showcases longer stories. I had the need to tell longer tales and the characters became more developed.

Now we stand at *Cooties*. Heh… *Cooties*. This book was going to be called "Wet Willies", but I found out that can mean something entirely different and somewhat more lurid in the UK. I love this book. For me, this one feels like everything just came together. It is the first time I chose to go the route of a continuing story line and that left me the room to go all out, rabid monkey style, which really lets Lenore shine. So, enough with the goblety gook. I hope you enjoy Lenore's adventures as much as I enjoyed making them. If not, too bad cause we all know it'll be like four more years before the next one comes out.

– Dirge

INTRODUCTION

Issue #9

For two years now, Nevermore has been peaceful and quiet ...and smelled 60% fresher.

LENORE

PLOP

WHY? OH WHY MUST THIS BEEE?

LENORE, I MISS YOU SO MUCH MY LITTLE ZOMBIE... WOOGUMS!

THIS PAST YEAR HAS BEEN...

... WELL, RELATIVELY PAINLESS PHYSICALLY,

BUT EMOTIONALLY I AM A SHELLED OUT SOUL SEARCHING. SEARCHING FOR MY SPIRITUAL... UM... NUT.

SCRATCH SCRATCH

IF I COULD TRADE PLACES WITH YOU, I WOULD DO SO IN AN...

WHACK!

I NEVER LIKED YOU.

UM...

COUGH! COUGH!

GASP!

BWA! ~

LENORE! YOU'RE ALIVE! ...SORTA.

MAN, YOU'RE STANKY!

I'VE BEEN SO ALONE UP THERE IN THE HOUSE.

THINGS COME OUT OF THE WALLS THERE AT NITE YOU KNOW!

THINGS!

I LIKE THINGS...

WHAT THE HELL IS THAT ANYWAY?

DOOKIE EATING-PIG LOV'N - CRAB LIKE - BOW LEGGED -
CREEPY ASS - BULBOUS HEADED - SMALLER THAN A BREAD BOX -
HOLLOW BRAINED - GOPHER LICK'N - INTESTINE SHAPED -
BACON WRAPPED - NO SOAP USING - SQUID SLURPING -
BOTCHILISM GROWING - CROTCH SCRATCHING - ONE BALLED -
ACCIDENTALLY BIRTHED - FILTH SPREADING -
JUICE PRODUCING - GREASY PALMED - FART LEAKING -
BALL OF CRAP SHAPED LIKE A LITTLE MAN.

WAIT A SEC.

WERE YOU IN THE AFTERLIFE?

YEEEAH, BUT IT WAS ITCHY AND SMELLED LIKE FRITOS THERE, SO I LEFT.

YOU... YOU JUST LEFT THE AFTERLIFE?

SURE. IT WAS NO BIGGIE. I DON'T THINK ANYONE EVEN NOTICED OR CARED.

YOU WILL FIND THE ESCAPED CHILD AND RETURN HER OR BE DESTROYED!

YES SIR!

poop!

UGHH

MY NOGGIN SURE GOT WHALLOPED!

AT LEAST THE PAIN IS STARTING TO SUBSIDE.

CHUNK!

OWWWW

I SEEK THE BLONDE GIRL CHILD!

GIMMIE!

OLD HOUSE ON THE HILL.

THANK YOU.

CAN I HAVE MY THINGY BACK?

SHLOOP

BLEGHH

BLEGHHH AH

UGHH... HERE PARK THE PINTO BACK IN THE GARAGE. MAN.

HEY.

CATCH!

AND THAT SMELL! IT'S SEEPING INTO MY PORES!

OH! OH! AND YOU... WAIT A MINUTE..

..YOU LIKE HIM DON'T YOU?

HE'S DREEEEAMY.

SMOOCH SMOOCH SMOOCH

YOU... YOU LIKE ME?

WILL YOU BE MY BOYFRIEND?

SHOVE!

ARE YOU KIDDING!?

OW! THAT HURT!

YOU DON'T KNOW WHAT THIS MEANS TO ME! I'LL WORSHIP YOU! I'LL BE THE BESTEST BOYFRIEND EVER. I'LL...

I HAVE FEELINGS LENORE AND YOU...

ZIP

WHAT THE! ARGHHHH

TINKLE TINKLE

Sometimes love is best buried deep.
...Like six feet deep.

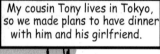

THINGS INVOLVING ME
THE EVIL URINAL

So I was in Japan with Jhonen and Steve (Steve is an Invader Zim director) on the day before Halloween 2000.

My cousin Tony lives in Tokyo, so we made plans to have dinner with him and his girlfriend.

UNFORTUNATELY, JHONEN GOT A LITTLE SICKY...

HEY! YOU COMING?

KNOCK KNOCK

SPLORCH BLOOBLE BLOOB PLOOKA PLOOK

*THOSE NOISES AIN'T COMING FROM A MOUTH

BEING REALLY HUNGRY AND WANTING TO EXPLORE, STEVE AND I STILL WENT.

We met up at a themed restaurant. It had two floors. The top was themed like Heaven. The bottom, like Hell. We, of course, went straight to Hell.

POP GOES THE WEASEL

'Round and 'round the cobbler's bench

WOO!

The monkey chased the weasel.

HA HA

WEEE

The monkey thought it was all in fun

POP goes the weasel !

POP

OH MY GOD! HOLD ON LITTLE BUDDY! HOLD ON!

DING DONG

PUMP PUMP

A penny for a spool of thread-
A penny for a needle...

ONE PENNY, EACH.

BUY THEM! I'LL FORM RUDIMENTARY STITCHES!

BUT I LIKE MY PENNIES.

Three months twelve days and two hours after the first story ended...

LENORE

The Cute Little Dead Girl.

#10

THIS ISSUE WILL ROCK YOUR NUTS!

You know, like a squirrel's nuts or something.

Issue #10

Mmmm... A nice cozy, lazy summer.

Just drink'n some juice with not a single problem to worry about. Just drink'n that juice there. ...no problem.

THEY'RE LOOSE!!

BOOM

WHAT?! WHAT'S LOOSE!

QUICK! THERE'S NO TIME!

OK, BUT WHAT? WHAT'S LOOSE!?

OH... HOW COULD THIS HAVE HAPPENED?

WHAT IS...

ZOOM

EEEK

EEK

TWO HOURS LATER

I... I MUST HAVE BLACKED OUT.

WHAT HAPPENED?

AW MAN, IT WAS GREAT. YOU SHOULD HAVE SEEN IT.

THE MICE WERE GOING TO TOWN ON YOU, TEARING YOU A NEW ONE.

WHEN THEY HAD RIPPED YOU COMPLETELY APART...

THEY SCURRIED ON... YET THEY HAD AN UNSATISFIED LOOK ON THEIR FACES.

AND AS NEAR AS I CAN FIGURE, SOMETHING LIKE THIS MUST'VE HAPPENED...

THE MICE GRABBED A CAB INTO TOWN...

WENT TO A BUTCHERS

BOUGHT SOME PIG INNARDS

TOOK A SEWING CLASS

CAME BACK. STUFFED YOU FULL OF PIG INNARDS—

SEWED YOU BACK UP

ATE A SANDWICH

MUNCH MUNCH

AND THEN SAVAGELY RIPPED OUT YOUR INNARDS!!

WOO BOY, YOU SHOULD'VE SEEN IT! WHAT A BEAUTY!!

OH, C'MON! THAT DID NOT HAPPEN!

AND HOW COME NOTHING HAPPENED TO YOU?

THEY TRIED TO GET ME RIGHT AFTER FEASTING OFF YOUR PIGGY GUTS.

ARGH!

THUNK

CLAK CLAK CLAK

SCABIES

An itchy condition of the skin caused by tiny MITES.
Usually burrows around male genitalia.

BUGGIES!

HEY, I THINK I SEE THE MEESES COMING BACK.

Bu.. Bu.. Bu..

YOUR CROTCH IS JUST LIKE TACO BELL.

BUT NOOOOO TACOS.

SHINGLES

A painful, blistering rash that affects one side of the body, making you surprisingly tired and depressed. Blisters will usually crust over and then burst.

THEY'RE GETT'N CLOSER.

WELL, I AINT TOUCHING LOBSTER BOY.

WE CAN'T JUST LEAVE HIM HERE.

MAYBE IF WE DRAG MR. MISERY HERE WITH A STICK.

NO ONE LOVES ME, I'M SO ALONE...

I FOUND THIS STICK, BUT IT HAS A BIG RUSTY NAIL IN IT.

WAIT WAIT... I FEEL BETTER. THE BLISTERS HAVE CRUSTED OVER.

YEAH, YOU LOOK...

...GREAT.

BOOM.

ARGHHHH

WHACK WHACK

LENORE!! HELP ME! USE YOUR OLD KNIFE!

NAH. I DON'T WANNA.

YEAHHHH... BUT SPOOKY LITTLE GIRLS WITH KNIVES HAS BECOME SO CLICHÉ THESE DAYS. I KEEP SEEING THEM NOW ON T-SHIRTS.

BUT... YOU USED TO LOVE THAT KNIFE!

NOW I USE MONKEY STICK.

OOK OOK

SQUEAK SQUEAKA SQUEAK!

TRANSLATION: THERE SHE IS, THE ONE WE'RE AFTER!

ARGHHHHHHH

I'M MAKING MY THINKING FACE.

SEVERAL YEARS AGO ....

Little Bunny Foo Foo
Hopping through the forest

Picking up little field mice ...

and...

...bopping them on the head.

BOOM

Ewwwww

SQUEAK! TRANSLATION: "FATHER!"

SQUEAK! TRANSLATION: "I WILL RAISE A MIGHTY ARMY TO VANQUISH THY BUNNY-LIKE ENEMY. NO MATTER HOW LONG IT TAKES, I SHALL AVENGE YOU FATHER!!!"

OH! CRAP! DEAD END!

TH...THEY'RE GONNA COME IN HERE AND THEY'RE GONNA GET US!

YUP. DOOMED.

WHAT? YOU HAVE THE GAS?

MY NAME IS OUCHIE BOO BOO. I AM YOUR LONG LOST TWIN SISTER WHO HAS COME TO HELP SAVE YOU FROM YOUR DARK MOUSEY FATE. DO YOU UNDERSTAND?

Meanwhile...

LENORE? POOTY?

WHERE'D THOSE GUYS GO? MAN, THIS DAY CAN'T GET ANY WORSE...

SCRATCHI-CROTCHI-ANAL-BURN -BURN-DRIPPY-CHUNK

A severely painful explosive discharge caused by tiny fanged demon pufferfish that dig through the male genitals, then lay large egg sacks that quickly hatch- spawning new demon pufferfish that quickly grow, mate through inbreeding, then lay more egg sacks, each time larger than the last. The cycle will continue until the victim is SO full of pufferfish, they explode outward through EVERY orifice from the pressure.

SPLOOM

ARGHHHAAA AAAA A A AAAAAAAA A A A AAURGLE AROOOOO...

WHAT THE HELL WAS THAT? SOUNDED LIKE A THOUSAND KITTENS SLOWLY DYING.

NO, THOSE SOUND DIFFERENT.

THE MICE HAVE ALL BEEN DEFEATED!

YOU TOOK THEIR FEET?

WHERE YA GOIN' SIS?

WANNA DO MAKEOVERS?

I'M JUST GOING TO GO FRESHEN UP BEHIND THAT BIG ROCK REAL QUICK.

AGENT OUCHIE BOO BOO IS IN POSITION. I HAVE THE ESCAPED CORPSE GIRL AND THE ROGUE BOUNTY HUNTER IN SIGHT. REQUESTING PERMISSION TO PERSONALLY ENGAGE IN CAPTURE.

NEGATIVE OUCHIE BOO BOO. THE GIRL SHOULD BE HARMLESS, BUT THE BOUNTY HUNTER, POOTY, IS EXTREMELY DANGEROUS. I AM SENDING THE TROOPS TO YOUR POSITION. NO DEAD SHALL EVER ESCAPE THE DEPTHS OF HECK EVER AGAIN!!

NEXT ISSUE:
BATTLE ROYALE

the GHOST AND THE SNAKE

There once was a little baby snake...

who was born long after his siblings. They, with their mother, had long since ventured off, assuming his egg was a dud.

MOMMY?

The baby snake wanted a mommy, but no one seemed willing.

Instead, they just seemed scared.

MOMMY?

Really scared.

MOMMY?

I mean, just look at that bug there.

MOMMY?!

The baby snake looked long and hard, but it was completely moot.

· Until one day he spotted a promising prospect.

MOMMY?

The baby snake was sure he had at last found his mommy.

The ghost had no arms, just like the baby snake.

Others were scared of the ghost, much like they were of the baby snake.

However, the ghost insisted the baby snake was wrong. The ghost is a floaty spectral creature, and the snake is a scaled living thing.

The ghost sent the baby snake on his way.

The baby snake was so busy pondering this, he did not see the car.

...And the baby snake was sure he had at last found his mommy.

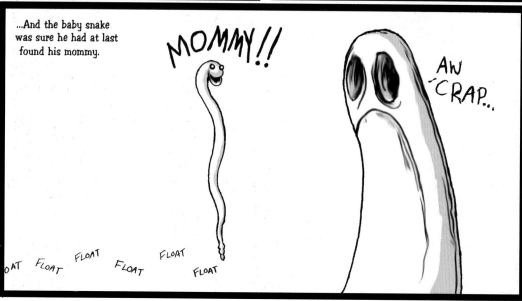

THINGS Involving ME
Young Roman

Issue # 11

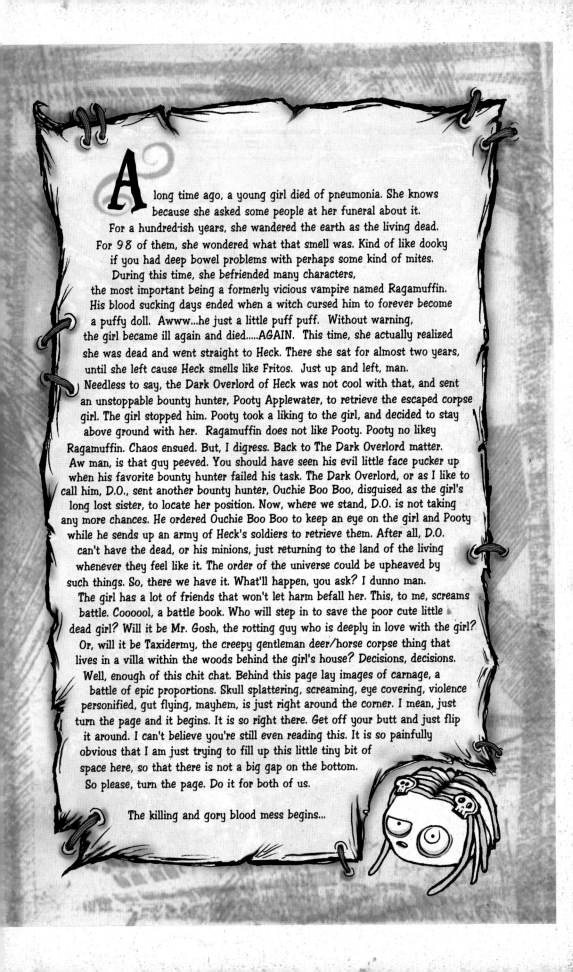

A long time ago, a young girl died of pneumonia. She knows because she asked some people at her funeral about it. For a hundred-ish years, she wandered the earth as the living dead. For 98 of them, she wondered what that smell was. Kind of like dooky if you had deep bowel problems with perhaps some kind of mites. During this time, she befriended many characters, the most important being a formerly vicious vampire named Ragamuffin. His blood sucking days ended when a witch cursed him to forever become a puffy doll. Awww...he just a little puff puff. Without warning, the girl became ill again and died.....AGAIN. This time, she actually realized she was dead and went straight to Heck. There she sat for almost two years, until she left cause Heck smells like Fritos. Just up and left, man. Needless to say, the Dark Overlord of Heck was not cool with that, and sent an unstoppable bounty hunter, Pooty Applewater, to retrieve the escaped corpse girl. The girl stopped him. Pooty took a liking to the girl, and decided to stay above ground with her. Ragamuffin does not like Pooty. Pooty no likey Ragamuffin. Chaos ensued. But, I digress. Back to The Dark Overlord matter. Aw man, is that guy peeved. You should have seen his evil little face pucker up when his favorite bounty hunter failed his task. The Dark Overlord, or as I like to call him, D.O., sent another bounty hunter, Ouchie Boo Boo, disguised as the girl's long lost sister, to locate her position. Now, where we stand, D.O. is not taking any more chances. He ordered Ouchie Boo Boo to keep an eye on the girl and Pooty while he sends up an army of Heck's soldiers to retrieve them. After all, D.O. can't have the dead, or his minions, just returning to the land of the living whenever they feel like it. The order of the universe could be upheaved by such things. So, there we have it. What'll happen, you ask? I dunno man. The girl has a lot of friends that won't let harm befall her. This, to me, screams battle. Coooool, a battle book. Who will step in to save the poor cute little dead girl? Will it be Mr. Gosh, the rotting guy who is deeply in love with the girl? Or, will it be Taxidermy, the creepy gentleman deer/horse corpse thing that lives in a villa within the woods behind the girl's house? Decisions, decisions. Well, enough of this chit chat. Behind this page lay images of carnage, a battle of epic proportions. Skull splattering, screaming, eye covering, violence personified, gut flying, mayhem, is just right around the corner. I mean, just turn the page and it begins. It is so right there. Get off your butt and just flip it around. I can't believe you're still even reading this. It is so painfully obvious that I am just trying to fill up this little tiny bit of space here, so that there is not a big gap on the bottom. So please, turn the page. Do it for both of us.

The killing and gory blood mess begins...

OH, OK. I...

EAT THE ⊙☆#BANANA!!

I DON'T WANT THE ⊙☆# BANANA!!

YOU'RE JUST NOT GONNA BEND ON THIS BANANA THING, ARE YOU?

LOOK, I'M SORRY. EVEN WHEN I DID USED TO EAT FOOD, I NEVER LIKED BANANAS, SO, YES. ON THIS, I MUST REMAIN FIRM.

YUP. FIRM.

...JUST LIKE A BANANA.

WOULD YOU PLEASE DROP IT!?

BUT... IT'LL GET GRASS ON IT.

WHY'S YOU WANNA GRASS MY BANANA?

I DON'T CARE ABOUT THE DAMN BANANA! I JUST WANT TO MOVE ALONG.

I... LOOK, I KNOW YOU ARE "SPECIAL" IN THE HEAD, SO I'M TRYING TO REMAIN VERY CAL...

SWEET JESUS!! JUST GIMMIE THE POOR BIRD!!!

C'MON... WHERE'D YOU STASH HIM? IS HE IN YOUR BUTT? HE'S IN YOUR BUTT, ISN'T HE?!

OH, SWEET INNOCENT LITTLE BIRDY... IF YOU CAN HEAR ME, POSSIBLY DEEP THERE IN RAGAMUFFIN'S BUTT, I LOVE YOU SO MUCH! I'LL DEVOTE MY LIFE TO FINDING AND PROTECTING YOU.

IT'S ALL JUST TOO MUCH TO BARE. :SOB: BOO HOO SOB SNIFF... SOB

IF.. IF THE BIRDIE WERE HERE NOW, IT WOULD PROBABLY BE DOING A LITTLE DANCE LIKE THIS...

JIG   JIG

AND.. AND... HE'D BE SINGING A SONG, MOST LIKELY LIKE THIS... "TWEET TWEETY TWEET" SNIFF SNIFF "TOOT TWEETLE TOOT" :SOB:

HIS FEATHERY TUSH, JUST ROCK'N OUT...

OH, COME ON!!

THERE ARE NO FRICKEN BIRDS!

MEANWHILE, DEEP IN THE STINKY BOWELS OF HECK...

I KNOW THE DARK OVERLORD WANTED TO SEND OUT A FULL DIVISION TO APPREHEND THE ESCAPED CORPSE GIRL AND THE BOUNTY HUNTER, BUT THE RULES OF DEATH ALLOW ONLY 3 TO EXIT.

YES, I KNOW. ONLY A BLOOD SACRIFICE, FROM THAT WELL OF SOULS THERE, WOULD FULLY OPEN THE GATES OF HECK, AND THE ODDS OF THAT HAPPENING ARE A ZILLION TO...

BLAT!

THAT... THAT WAS AN ACCIDENT! YOU HAVE TO SEE THAT! I JUST WANTED THAT BANANA AS FAR AWAY FROM ME AS POSSIBLE. DON'T HURT ME.

PLEASE PLEASE!

IT WAS JUST A BIRD, MAN.

I AM SO CONFUSED.

SCRATCH SCRATCH

WHERE THE HECK DID YOU GUYS GO?

WE'S WENT TO GET CHICKEN.

CHICKEN CHICKEN

LENORE AND I WERE IN THE MIDDLE OF A TALK. I DON'T THINK SHE NEEDS TO BE BOTHERED BY...

CHICKENS GO BOK BOK BOK!

I.. *PANT PANT* HAD TO DO IT. *PANT*

IT HURT...

HEY, LOOK AT THIS NEAT THING.

WELL OF SOULS

OH... WAIT A MINUTE...

LL OF

I'M SURE I DON'T EVEN NEED TO BRING THIS UP, BUT THAT IS THE WELL OF SOULS, A DIRECT PIPELINE TO HECK. IF ONE DROP OF BLOOD GOES IN IT, THE DOOR SWINGS WIDE OPEN. THAT WOULD BE SO AWFUL. *SHUDDER*

BUT LIKE I SAID, I'M SURE IT'S NOT WORTH MENTIONING. THE ODDS OF ONE OF YOU THROWING BLOOD DOWN IT MUST BE A ZILLION TO...

SHLOOP

SHLOOP

SHLOOP

SHLOOP

WE'RE SCREWED.

WHAT? THEY'RE JUST LITTLE GOOEY EGGY SACKS WITH LITTLE PEOPLE IN THEM. THEY'RE KINDA CU...

CONTINUED NEXT ISSUE

NATURE'S REALLY AMAZING STUFF!

Nature is full of magical wonders. The Grand Canyon. Lightning. Jessica Simpson's career.

ARE CHICKENS TUNA? I SEEN A BUFFALO ONCE. BUY PIZZA AND MINTS. I THINK I JUST POOPED IN MY HEAD.

OH GAWD... OF ALL THE PEOPLE THEY COULD HAVE IMPLANTED ME IN...

One of the niftiest has to be that of the the insect "Phyllium Giganteum".

PHILIGANKAWHATA?

Well, more commonly known as "The Walking Leaf".

OH, HEY - THANKS FOR TAKING IT DOWN A NOTCH THERE TRIGGER. I KNOW I'M JUST A LOWLY LEAFY THING AND ALL, BUT I'LL TRY TO KEEP UP WITH YOUR FANCY PANTS, BOOK LEARN'N WAYS. ALSO, JUST F.Y.I, I'M MORE OF A "CRAWLING LEAF". I'D LOOK ODD WALKING AROUND ALL "DOO DEE DOO"

HEE HEE, I'M SLICK.

This natural camouflage works great in some surroundings.

HEE HEE, I'M SLICK.

Other surroundings, not so much.

Having friends can be difficult.

Embarrassing accidents may surface from time to time.

Sometimes, other accidents can happen to the detriment of all parties involved.

But, with the exception of those few drawbacks, A leaf bug lives a great life, protected by its amazing camouflage.

And...uh...

END

#12
Lenore
The cute little DEAD GIRL.
by
Roman Dirge

Issue #12

,AND MAYBE EVEN LOVED HIM TOO.

I...

BLURGLE?

HE'S MOVIN'!!

BAP
BAP
BAP
BAP

CLICK
CLICK

THUNK
THUNK
THUNK
THUNK

WHERE DID YOU GET THAT?!

I... I DON'T KNOW, *PANT* *PANT*

DID I HEAR GUNFIRE?

YEAH, I.. HEYYYY!!!

HELLO! I'M FLASHBACK SQUIRREL. THE NEXT 2 PANELS ARE FOR OUR CHEAP ASS FRIENDS WHO DIDN'T BUY ISSUE #11.

WEEEEEE

GOODBYE FRIENDS... NOW I GO ON THE LONG SLEEEEEE

NOOOOOO

I THOUGHT YOU WERE GOING ON "THE LONG SLEEP."

I DID! I SLEPT LIKE AN HOUR. THAT'S A LONG TIME FOR A DEMON.

SO, I SEE YOU GAVE THE DEMON SOLDIERS A BIG CAN OF WHOOP ASS. LOTTA BODIES OUT FRONT. WHAT'S OUR PLAN TO DEAL WITH THE REST OF THEM?

WHAT REST OF THEM? I KILLED THEM ALL.

YOU IDIOT. HECK'S ARMIES ARE IMMEASURABLE. THEY'LL JUST KEEP SENDING MORE. WE HAVE TO CLOSE THE PORTAL.

OH, PLEASE. I THINK I KNOW A LITTLE ABOUT HECK, AND I SAY FOR THE TIME BEING...

WE'VE SEEN THE LAST OF HECK'S SOLDIERS.

THAT'S IT. I'M CALLING IN THE SPAM WITCH.

THE WHAT?

HELLO!

HOLY CRAP I WANNA PLAY WITH THAT THING!

HI, POOTY! WHAT CAN I DO FOR YOU?

HOWDY, SPAM WITCH! I NEED YOUR AMAAAAAZING KNOWLEDGE. I NEED A WAY TO CLOSE AN OPEN PORTAL TO HECK OR ME AND MY PALS ARE ALL DOOMED TO SOME... DOOM, I GUESS. CAN YOU HELP ME? YOU KNOW, FOR OLD TIMES SAKE?

YOU UH... YOU NEVER RETURNED ANY OF MY CALLS, I THOUGHT WE WERE STILL GONNA BE FRIENDS AFTER THAT NIGHT.

WE ARE STILL FRIENDS, BABY. I'VE JUST BEEN REALLY BUSY WITH WORK AND STUFF. THE PROBLEM'S ME, NOT YOU.

BUT... I MADE YOU WAFFLES.

I KNOW YOU DID, BABY. I KNOW YOU DID.

NEAT Spells and stuff
And one cajun chicken recipe

THE ANSWER YOU SEEK LAY WITHIN THIS BOOK. NOW I MUST BE GOING.

OK. THAT WAS ... ODD. ALSO A LITTLE TOO MUCH INFO. ABOUT YOUR PRIVATE LIFE.

FLIP FLIP FLIP

L

HERE, I FOUND THE HECK PORTAL SECTION. READ IT AND TELL ME WHAT TO DO!

I JUST LOOKED OUT THE WINDOW!

K.

THERE'S AT LEAST A 100 SOLDIERS!

WE CAN'T WIN!

OK. APPARENTLY, YOU NEED TO MAKE RABID LOVE TO A GOAT WHILE WEARING A SUN DRESS AND HAT.

RIGHT!

WAIT, WHAT?

THAT'S WHAT IT SAYS! LOOK!

SIGH... FINE.

EVEN IF HE DOES CLOSE THE PORTAL, THERE'S STILL ABOUT 100 DEMONS OUT THERE WITH GUNS AND TANKS. I CAN'T FIGHT THEM ALL AND STILL PROTECT YOU. WE NEED BACK UP, BUT WHO, AND HOW?

YOU ARE NOW PROTECTED! WOOOO!!!

HEY, I TOTALLY REMEMBER YOU SORT OF!

YOU'RE MRS. MISSY SASSYBOTTOM, RIGHT?!

MR. CHIPPY.

EXACTLY!

UH... YEAH. SORRY I TOOK SO LONG TO GET HERE. I WALK FUNNY AND MY LEGS CHAFE ME IN THE GROIN A BIT. YOU SHOULD SEE THE RED BUMPS THAT...

NO, NO. THAT'S OK. HOW DID YOU KNOW WE NEEDED HELP ANYWAY?

I JUST WANT TO SEE THE BUMPS, MAN.

TAXIDERMY SAW WHAT'S HAPPENING FROM THE WOODS OUT BACK. HE PUT OUT A CALL TO ARMS.

WELL, I APPRECIATE YOU COMING, BUT NO OFFENSE, I DON'T THINK YOU CAN REALLY HELP US WITH...

BOOM

Dirge

Hickory Dickory Dock

TA-DA!

I DID IT! WOOOOO! I ROCK!

So... IS THAT IT THEN?

WHAT DO YOU MEAN?

NO, I MEAN... IT WAS REAL GREAT. YOU RAN UP AND DOWN A CLOCK. I DON'T KNOW IF YOU EARNED YOUR OWN JINGLE FOR IT.

OK, LOOK. I'M ON THE CLOCK NOW, CLIMBED RIGHT UP. TOOK ME 'BOUT 4 SECONDS. DO I GET MY OWN SONG NOW FOR IT?

WELL, MAYBE. I... I DON'T...

LOOK, I'M JUST SAYING SPICE IT UP A BIT.

HOW SO?

I THINK THE OBVIOUS THING TO DO IS JUGGLE THESE FIRE STICKS WHILE HULA-HOOPING.

YUP. NOW JUST RUN UP THE CLOCK WHILE DOING THAT.

I.. I'M NOT SUCH A GOOD JUGGLER. IS THIS GOOD?

8.4 seconds later...

SO, THAT'S IT THEN? YOU'RE JUST GONNA BE DEAD AND FLOAT UP ALL GHOSTY?

I F@#ING HATE YOU!

·END·

Things Involving Me

Bergen, Norway.
My artist friend Lise and I were bar hopping.
Everything was going great.
Time of my life.

THAT BAR WAS REALLY COOL. WHERE WE GONNA GO NE...

Until...

THIS HAPPENED!

OGLEY BLOOG RAK MOG?!!

ARGHHHH!

CENSORED

CENSORED

*IT WAS IN NORWEGIAN, SO "OGLEY BLOOG" IS WHAT I HEARD.

OG FLORGY MIK MAK?

She was wearing a naked suit made of stockings and waving scissors.

It was scary.

I... I DON'T KNOW WHAT YOU'RE SAYING. I...

CENSORED

OGLEY BLOOG RAK MOG!!!

OH, GOD! JUST TAKE MY MONEY!

CENSORED

SHES SAYING SHE WANTS TO CUT OFF YOUR UNDERWEAR TAG AND KEEP IT.

BUT I'D RATHER SHE DIDN'T.

OGLEY BLOO RAK MOG!

ARGHHHH

CENSORED

So I let her do it.

SNIP

CENSORED

CENSORED

ALRIGHT, IT'S... IT'S OVER. MY HEART COULD'NT HAVE TAKEN ONE MORE SECOND OF...

OGLEY BLOOG RAK MOG?

UH, ROMAN...

CENSORED

CENSORED

END

BEHOLD! I AM EVIL INCARNATE! FEAR MY VERY PRESENCE. TREMBLE FROM MY PURE BEAR DEADY-NESS! SHAKE, DAMN YOU! SHAKE!

UH, HUH. MAYBE LATER. BUSY EATING GRAPES.

BUT... I'M EVIL TRAPPED IN A STUFFED BODY. DOES THAT NOT TERRIFY YOU? HUH?

Yeahhh... NO. I'VE GOT ONE OF THOSE ALREADY, SO... YOU KNOW.

OH.

CAN I AT LEAST HAVE ONE GRAPE?

NO.

OH... I SEE. WELL, THEN, I GUESS I'll JUST BE ON MY W...

MUNCH MUNCH MUNCH

HI THERE! I'M SUPER HAPPY FLUFFY SUNSHINE BEAR, AND I...

ARGHHHHHHH

BAM BAM BAM BAM

DIE, FOUL BEASTIE! DIE!!!

MORAL: NEVER ASK ROMAN TO DO A CHARACTER CROSSOVER. END

Lenore

the cute little dead girl

Art by other peeps...

Eeeeeeeeeeeeevil peeps

steven Daily.o5

Yo, Roman! All joking aside, thanks for letting me be a part of Lenore!
I'm a big fan! Cheers! Voltaire